W9-AYR-775

J                                    474632
170.2                                9.95
Gol
Goley
Learn the value of
   responsibility

| DATE DUE | | | |
|---|---|---|---|
| | | | |
| | | | |
| | | | |
| | | | |
| | | | |
| | | | |
| | | | |
| | | | |
| | | | |
| | | | |
| | | | |
| | | | |

LEARN THE VALUE OF

# Responsibility

by ELAINE P. GOLEY

Illustrated by Dorey E. Evans

ROURKE ENTERPRISES, INC.
VERO BEACH, FL 32964

**Library of Congress Cataloging-in-Publication Data**

Goley, Elaine P., 1949–
    Learn the value of responsibility.

    Summary: Discusses areas in which individuals have
responsibility, such as homework, taking care of pets,
and helping family members.
    1. Responsibility—Juvenile literature.
[1. Responsibility]   I. Title.
BJ1451.G65   1988      170′.2′0222        88-4435
ISBN 0-86592-394-9

# Responsibility

Do you know what **responsibility** is?

**Responsibility** is taking care of your pets.

Doing your homework is your **responsibility** as a student.

**Responsibility** is helping your parents
do chores around the house.

You have a **responsibility** to be loyal to your friends.

**Responsibility** is practicing your piano lessons.

You have a **responsibility** to do your best
on the team.

When you're home alone, you have the **responsibility**
of doing what your parents want you to do.

**Responsibility** is doing the errands your mom asks you to do.

When you have a paper route, your **responsibility**
is to get the papers to each customer on time.

We have **responsibility** for helping our family when they need us.

**Responsibility** means behaving well in public.

When you answer the phone, you have the
**responsibility** for taking messages if your
parents aren't home.

You have **responsibility** for looking after your sister and brother.

It's your **responsibility** to brush
your teeth after every meal.

**Responsibility** is returning your
library books on time.

You are **responsible** for taking good care of your friend's bike when you ride it.

**Responsibility** is taking care of yourself and others by doing what you should.

# Responsibility

Amy and Mike were walking home from school.

"Let's roller skate when we get home," said Mike.

"I can't," said Amy. "I have homework to do and I promised my sister that I'd help her with math."

When she got home, Amy did her homework. "Okay," she said to her sister. "Now I can help you with your math."

How did Amy show **responsibility** for her homework? . . . For her sister?

How can you show that you take **responsibility**?

# Responsibility

It was a beautiful Saturday in October. Mark and Billy were riding their bikes through the colorful falling leaves.

"Let's ride down to the store," said Billy.

"Maybe tomorrow," said Mark. "I have to get home now. Mom wants me to rake the leaves."

Mark rode his bike home and put it in the garage so that it wouldn't get rusty if it rained. Then he got out the rake and started raking the leaves in the front yard. He raked until he had gathered up all the leaves and put them in bags.

How did Mark show he was **responsible**?
How did he take **responsibility** for his bike?
How can you show that you're **responsible**?